TOGETHER

LETS SURVIVE 20S

VISHRUTA DHOLAKIA

Made with ♥ on the Notion Press Platform
www.notionpress.com

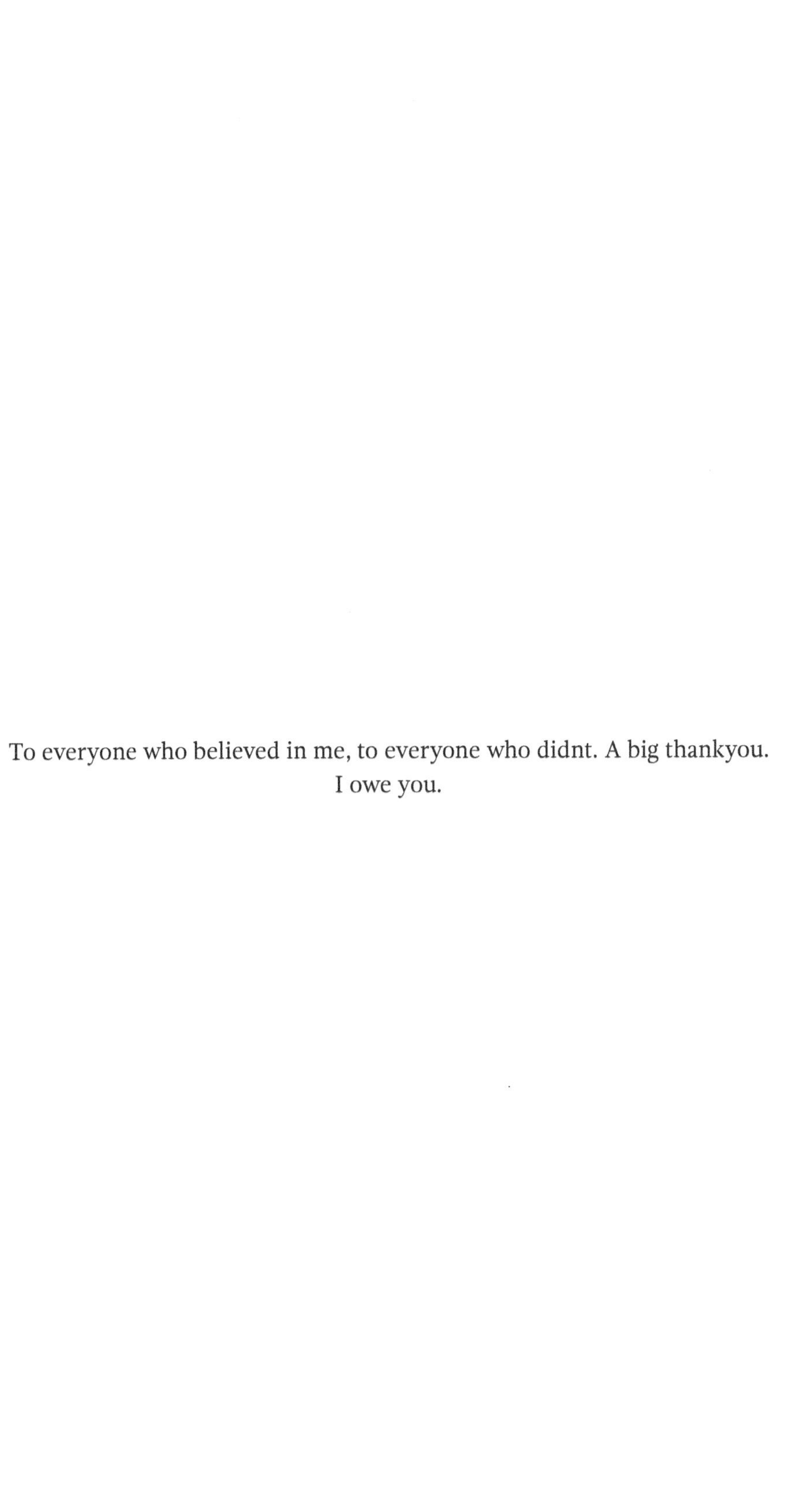

To everyone who believed in me, to everyone who didnt. A big thankyou.
I owe you.

Contents

Contents

Acknowledgements

I am grateful to each one of you- friends, family, supporters, rebels, and you my readers.

I thank my mom and dad, genuinely, for always believing in me and for all the support and love. It means a lot. I wouldnt be here if it wasnt for you.

I would like to take a minute and thank people whose philosophies, lessons and presence contiune to be my light in the lows- Devarshi Pandya, Fatema Kapasi, Pinali Rupareliya, Jenil Makati and Nishit Wadhwani.

And to people who stoody by, through thick and thin, guiding me- Param Meswania, Devashish Joshi, Durgesh Jadeja, Vedanshu Rajput.

Special thankyou and a big jappi to my sister- Titirsha, who has done innumerable efforts to cheer me up at in all my phases. ily.

God knows how many times there were disagreements with almost every name mentioned, but, for what I know is, every moment taught me some thing and so we here we are, wirting this book.

Prologue

I am beginning to write, today when my heart feels lighter than ever, when my power of imagination or senses as we say might or might not be upto the criteria of the perfect poetry/prose. but it sure will be a part of me. a part of me that is real, not fancied, not masked. only honesty and raw truth. It might lead you to laugh and cry and teach you to love and live, this book is not just a book, its a journey, of you and me, make sure you are engrossed in it as much as a kid might be when he gets his magical beans.

CHAPTER I

Pause; Look Around.

Wake up, hustle for that job, work overnight,
   cancel that party you wanted to go to since long,
   complicate the life by not saying out your heart.
   Do we ever pause for a moment?
   To look back and realise that time is passing by and the quote, life is
short, is coming true.
   Pause; look around.
   Cherish the colors, flowers, scents, and people around you.
   grab that boy and kiss him. Tell him you love him,
   go to that party you were waiting for,
   go eat that food, try, explore and discover, but above all,
   Take a break. you and me, and everyone deserves it.

CHAPTER II

This human is you.

When you are in your 20s, trying to live the life while you have died every single day, dont give into your fears. Overcome them. A small step each day. Renew that gym membership, push a little bit harder today. Go to that party, you were going to skip because of work. No, because these are the moments you will remember. These are the days you will cherish and celebrate forever. Live your 20s. And not just 20s, you will never be this young as you are today.

Yes I know, this is something google and instagram feeds calls us out on everyday. But this is different. Same words except that these advices are from a human who has outgrown over a year. A human who is trying to live the life and not get caught up in complications. This human is you. You the one reading this.

CHAPTER III

Doǹt think zyada

"but this is not for me, they will laugh on me mumma."

"I wish I could make you realise, that you are beautiful. And what ***they*** *say will **never** change anything about you. Precisely, it says a lot more about them and lot less about you.* "

And your mumma says, "dont think zyada".

CHAPTER IV

Preparing for life

When she asks you to wear/do/make what might make you feel uncomfortable, isnt that what we call, *preparing for life* ? Isn`t that her way of saying, "**I know you are strong enough to overcome this. and even if you dont, I will still love you the same or even more.**"

But how is it so, that by our 20s we forget, to love this self of us, that our mumma and papa took care of really well ?

CHAPTER V

Very wrong Ego

I remember, when I was in my to be an adult phase of my life, I could not ever possibly think of myself. All I cared about was the love from others, those others who never actually were meant to give me love.

I kept begging (not literally) but yes, love from everyone else but me, mattered the most to me. And I kept running around in search of it, shifting different group of friends who would serve me love inconsistently, going out with different boys who themselves werent sure what kind of haircut they want to get, and its not wrong, you know. Going out, meeting different people just for the sake of it, is not wrong. What was wrong was, the motive behind it. I wanted my ego to be fullfilled. Which was wrong, VERY WRONG.

CHAPTER VI

Within-

If I could go back in time, ever, I would tell myself to look for love, *WITHIN* . There is no better home than you yourself.

Every other people you expect love from, are also like you. A lot like you. They are also figuring out their lives like you are.

"Would'nt it be unfair to ask them to give you everything that you are struggling to give it to yourselves as well ?"

CHAPTER VII

Nahi, you can not.

And maybe, if you and me, gave that love to ourselves, as much as we give to others, it would be all cherries and cakes.

Those "chances" you are willing to give to others, save them for you. Use them for you.

See, becuase when you are so involved with figuring out the right way to be an adult, whilst living whilst making money, whilst expecting your love life to be all sorted, there comes a point when you realise that there is no right way to do life. there is only your way to do life. *Nahi,* you can not expect your life to be a steep rise, it wont ever be. nor will it be a steep fall. If it rises, it will fall. If it falls, it will rise. Every time.

CHAPTER VIII

Nothing is special.

With the October at its end,
    I guess it is safe to say that
    we all learned life a little more this year.
    Not just this year, we learn the bit of life every day.
    Yess but what is so special about it this year?
    Nothing ,

Not you alone.

except, that, this year,
   you will acknowledge this change,
   not you alone, but along with me, and maybe a thousand readers who are reading this right now.

Life Happens.

From all the lessons we were made to learn,
    the most basic thing I learned is, that, life happens.
    To each and every one of us, life happens.
    it could be positive or it couldnt.
    But, one thing`s for sure, you will survive. We all do.
    No matter, how breatheless your cries are right now,
    one day, sun will shine brighter for you, than all of us.
    I have said it before but I will say it again,

*"There is no specific guide to wing the life, there is only **your way.**"*

You cry, laugh, supress, depress, but at the end, you get through with it.
    Call it strength, fate, faith, or LIFE.
    You choose whichever way you want. there is no right ot wrong.
    why do i repeatedly say this? Well, hammer your brain. Stop looking for advices in the videos,reels or grams. Find it within yourself. I think, its more like hit and trial, rather than a wild hunt.

CHAPTER XI

You and you and you

your memories, your laugh in the winter, your giggle in the summer after noon, your smile in the fall, your soggy feet in the rain, your yawns, your snores, your face of the sleep, your hugs, your old tee-shirt, your obsession for the color red, your sulky moodswings, your calls, your "lets meet" texts, the lavish fragrance of your happiness, you and you and you and you.

but, today, I let go. I choose to free myself from you, because you, left a long time back, and today is the time, I pick myself and strive for all the growth I wish I could have.

trash

Because, let me tell you, that it is possible. It is possible to be that girl, to be that gym shark you always wanted to be, but couldnt, because the best thing we did back then was to cry on the bathroom floors, because you cant do it anymore. You are helpless. Your heart loves him, your mind is tired of the tiny little arguments of everyday, that you can not do it anymore. But you can not let go of him because then, who will love you. because what if this is exactly what you deserve. Because, what if, he is the love of your life.

trash. yes, let me be your mother for a while, and hear me out.

How on Earth

This is not love. This could be anything else, but love. And I am sad, that you are made to believe that, violence is love. I wish I could make you feel what Love really is.

look in the mirror

How on this earth, this human deserves THIS? itsnt it cruel?

Its not them, its you.

Took me long to realise, its not them, its you.
    Its you who sees pretty,
    even though they have shown you,
    who they are.
    It always had been hard for me to accept,
    the truth, the reality, the facts,
    quite visible to everyone else but me.
    Guess, I decoded the flaw,
    We have pink eyes, or, we wear pink glasses.
    We all have romanticised everything in itself.

"The code-? See people for who they are. And not who you think they are / expect them to be."

Seriously, A boy?

Look at the pattern. He broke your heart. He cheated on you. The another he came, broke you, hurt you and took all his love and went away.

Are you telling me, that, you are so petty enough to be broken by a boy?? seriously? A BOY?

Toh ab?

You know, within you that, you are stronger, you are more than the compliments he gives (the emojis are not compliments though:/), you know, you deserve much more love than he gives you.

I am not saying, Everyone is Perfect. Infact, I am saying the exact opposite. Everyone around you, associated with you or not, has red flags. RED SIGNS. The signs that you are to analyse. Instead of ignoring.

Listen, queen? everyone you meet, be it friend, boyfriend, girlfriend, parents, relatives, sisters, brothers, everyone has red flags.

Toh ab?

CHAPTER XVII

Butterflies/ Red flags ?

No way you can nulify the red flags. All you can do is, analyse which behavior, which pattern, which tactic affects you in what way.

Your body sends you signals. When there is a negative energy around you, body sends signals. Yes, your body sends you signals, alerts you, warns you. But well we? We think they are **butterflies.**

"The butterflies are not love. They are a way of your body calling you out on negative energy. "

you are safe.

Bhai, meri baat sun,

The shiverings, the nervousness, the sweat, the bloating stomach are NOT butterflies.

When you love someone, they make you feel comfortable. Most of the times, when people fall in love, the research says, they do not feel nervous. That is your body telling you, that, you are safe.

"I just do"

they ask, "Why do you love him?"
she says, "I just do !"

Why him/her?

Nahi, this is not the most romantic answer. This is not "she loves me selflessly".

Tell me something, *bachpan mein* you had your favourite car? You were asked Why this car, You said, it looks much like the ferrari you saw in the movie with *abba.*

Even when you were a kid, you had an answer to why this. as stupid and naive it might be, but you had an answer. *haina?*

To fir, how come after growing up, when somebody asks you why him/her, you have no answer?

CHAPTER XXI

Do you trust me?

Do you trust me?
batao?
If its a yes, hear me, This is not love. The sorrys, please, gifts, cookies, will not soothe your broken relationship with that guy. He needs to fix himself before he could fix anything. That feeling, you call love is often misunderstood.

Its what psychology calls, Emotional Attachment.

The attachment is never love. Not just Psychology, but, Bhagvadgita says, Love is Free.

"When you love someone, you set them free."

This Emotional Attachment that you have developed, is not good for you. let go.

CHAPTER XXII

Underlying Psychology.

What are the signs that it is not love?

- You feel anxious when your partner is away.
- You worry about them cheating on you.
- You feel restless when they are busy.
- You feel lonely if your partner is not home.
- You constantly feel the need to ask about their whereabouts.

These are just the common signs. Basically the underlying Psychology is, you depend on your partner for your happiness. You depend on them too much to a point it suffocates you both.

He is worried and its my duty to make him happy. girl. listen, it is not. He is a man. and boys? She is a woman. They are mature enough to cheer themselves up.

I am not saying, you should not be there for your partner. But being there for them, doesnt mean, you will be anxious.

Be there for them. Help them. Dont pressurise yourself because they are in worry.

"It is nobody`s duty but ours to make ourselves happy."

CHAPTER XXIII

Read Bible?

"Bible says, Love never fails. And if it fails, it never was love."

Sometimes they leave,not because they did not love you, but because, their freedom was threatened. And believe me, everyone wants to be free. If you were them, you`d do the same.

And, you realise it or not, it is suffocating for you too. You will realise it once they are gone. And you are forced to not know what they are doing and where they are. You eventually feel a sense of freedom inside you.

Generally, it doesnt mean, they suffocated you. It might sometimes, you choked yourself with your unhealthy patterns.

CHAPTER XXIV

Coffee?

Too much to digest?
    Take a break. Come back to this page later.
    Put the books aisde. Have a coffee. And sit silence.
    Think what i am trying to say.

CHAPTER XXV

f*ck it !

Hi ! Again, I am glad, you came back. lets restart?

Most of the times, its nobody`s fault. You love them too much to let them go. You are too scared to see them falling for someone else, you are too afraid of getting close to them, because what if they leave you?

but, baby, what if they will?

No one will love you?

fuck it.

CHAPTER XXVI

I love you.

I will love you. Your family loves you. Your dog loves you The cat you are feeding the food to loves you. And, even if nobody loves you. I will.

I see you, trying to learn. I see you. You are getting there and i love you for whatever you are and for whatever you are not.

Listen, dont stress. Calm down. Digest everything one by one. I am sure, you will.

CHAPTER XXVII

Its so simple.

Most of the times when they love you, and you love them, you have a concrete reason.

Somebody asks you why? You have a reason. It can be so simple like he is a kid with me/ he lets me be me.

But hey, you do have a reason always. And it doesnt mean you have selfish reasons to love them. It just means, you know what you want and why you want.

And that is smart. That is mature.

CHAPTER XXVIII

It gets better.

Sometimes, despite of all the efforts and despite of everything, we are made to live without them. it just does not work out. Now whose fault is that?

Nobody`s.

That just means, you were not perfect for each other.

He is not wrong. Nor are you. Just the time isnt right. And probably, you werent meant to be.

And no matter, what you do, there isnt anything you can do about it. You take the love, memories and sometimes lessons, along with you, and carry them in your heart forever.

You move on to a better place. But that doesnt mean, the old memories just lash out. They dont.

I could have told you, that time heals. It doesnt. The truth is, it doesnt heal and hell, sometimes, it does not heal too. You just learn to live with it. You learn to love them from afar. You learn to be okay with them being gone. You make peace with it. And that happens, over years. But what I am sure of is,

"Whatever happens to you, with you, always has a reason behind it. You have to have faith and patience to know whats in the box for you. "

Dont pressurize yourself to be okay immediately. Let it happen. Dont bottle up your feelings.

"Say what you have to, feel what you have to."

you were happy-

How do you accept? The person who was so dearly to you is not in your life anymore? You were happy. Satisifed. Like nothing could whack you anymore.

Trust me with this one, I have been through this feeling too. But, tell me something, would you like a stagnant life? Because I wouldnt. And, I guess you too, would want anything but a stagnant life.

You were happy. Yes I know.

But the lesson I learned the hard way? When you love someone, you set them free. It doesnt mean they have to be with you, they have to be in a RELATIONSHIP with you or vice versa to feel loved you dont need a RELATIONSHIP.

You admire them. You can do it from afar. You respect them, you can do it, even with them being gone.

you v/s you

You were good before them. You will be better after them.

Thats the difference, When you have an emotional attachment, it is difficult for you to let go. You think their existence is your existence. Their absence from your life ruins everything.

NO, Bhai it doesnt.

Your existence is yours.

People are just lessons. Some stay. some dont. They make your life easier, sometimes they dont.

but, thats it. Its always you v/s you. ALWAYS.

CHAPTER XXXI

You got it!

hey, hey, I know it sucks. You are not alone. Its not just you who is going through heartbreaks, betrayals, tough times, rough times, but whole of the universe is with you. Somewhere, you are sharing the same pain as others. And that exactly what makes it easier.

Learn to control your mind. Think good. THINK.

Feel whatever you haveto, to get better. Rage. Pain. Kindness.Desperateness. EVERYTHING. but eventually,

hold tight! and, look at that bigger picture. You will grow older. you would have achieved everything that you want. good job, dream car, big house, muscular body, everything. you are getting married to a man of your dreams. they are getting married. you wish them luck/ you both meet again and click .

So, there are endless number of possiblities. Just learn to think right. Have faith. Look at the bigger picture. Ask yourself , if this thing will affect you in a year. If not, let it go. If yes, do something about it. If things are not in your control, dont stress. You got it.

I am there. We all are there for you, with you. I Love you. Dont stress out. Live.

Inspired By-

- *Selena Gomez*

- *Rupi Kaur*

- *Megha Rao*